Scuba Matt's Underwater Adventure

Written By
Echo Morgan

Illustration By
Anastasia Moshkarina

In Loving Memory of Matt Morgan

Your love of the ocean and passion for scuba diving

remains with those you have touched and taught.

May this book inspire future divers and protectors of the ocean.

From birth, man carries the weight of gravity on his shoulders.
He is bolted to earth. But man has only to sink beneath the surface and he is free.

- Jacques Yves Cousteau

Follow us for news of new books and giveaways at RedFinBooks.com
or @RedFinBooks on Instagram and Facebook.

Author: Echo Morgan
Ilustrator: Anastasia Moshkarina
Some elements of this book were designed using resources from Freepik.com

Library of Congress Control Number: 2020925608
ISBN   978-1-7360291-2-1

Copyright © 2020
All rights reserved. No part of this book may be reproduced, distributed, or transmitted in any form or by any means, including photocopying, recording, or other electronic or mechanical methods, without the prior permission of the author, except in the case of brief quotations embodied in critical articles or reviews.

The moral right of Echo Morgan to be identified as the author of this book has been asserted by me in accordance with the Copyright, Designs and Patents Acts 1988.

For permission requests visit: RedFinBooks.com

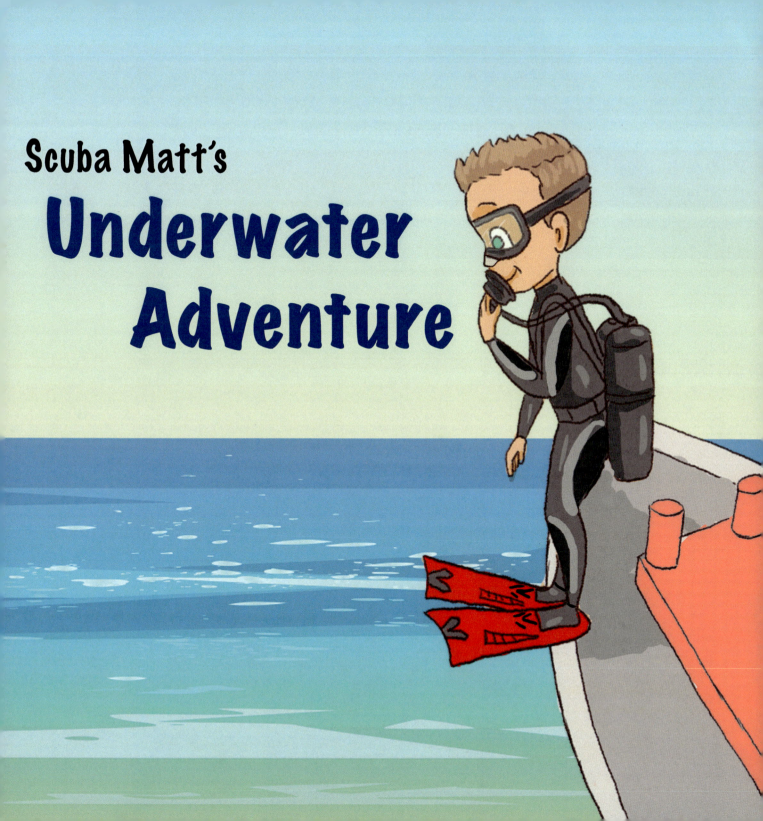

Hello, my name is Matt and I'm a scuba instructor.
I love exploring the ocean and all its wonder.

Come along on this underwater adventure with me,
and you will be amazed at all the things we will see.

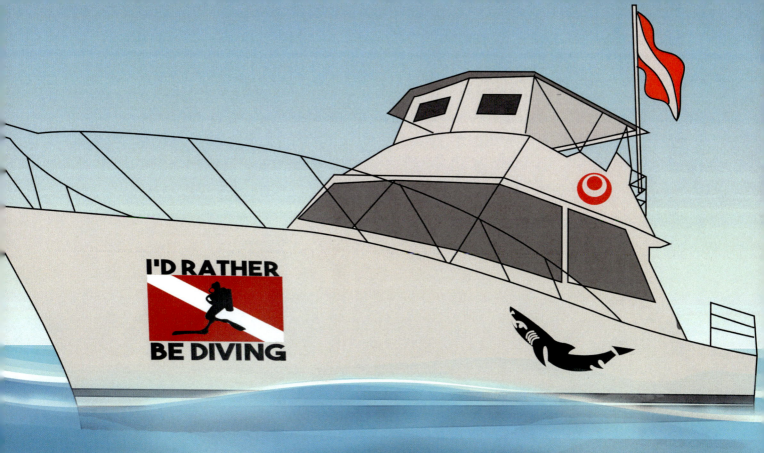

Did you know? Scuba divers use special gear to breathe underwater. Scuba stands for **S**elf-**C**ontained **U**nderwater **B**reathing **A**pparatus.

Ready, down into the warm blue water we go.
The first thing we see is coral reef down below.

The sea is filled with things we've never seen before.

Keep an eye out for turtles, octopus and more.

Did you know?
A coral reef is like an underwater city. Many sea animals use the coral reef as a home and food source.

Check out the reef! A school of clownfish swim around. They're hiding in anemone, so they're not found.

One peeks out curiously. Does he want to play?

A scuba diver has come to visit today.

Did you know? All clownfish are born male. Some become female later in life.

An angelfish and his friends are swimming my way.

They swim so close as if they have something to say.

One angelfish is swimming near to check me out.
But then changes course with a quick turnabout.

Did you know?
Angelfish are very curious and have been known to swim near scuba divers.

Over near the reef is a special and rare sight.
A yellow seahorse with its tail curled up tight.

He holds his horse-shaped head up high. His tail is down. He uses his tiny back fin to glide around.

Did you know? Seahorses can look forward and backward at the same time.

Look down there in the sand. A brightly colored star. Sea stars move slowly. It won't get very far.

A sea star is very interesting to study. His mouth is on the underside of his body.

Did you know? Some species of sea stars have 10, 20, and even 40 arms.

The endless sand below is full of fun surprises.
With seashells of so many different shapes and sizes.

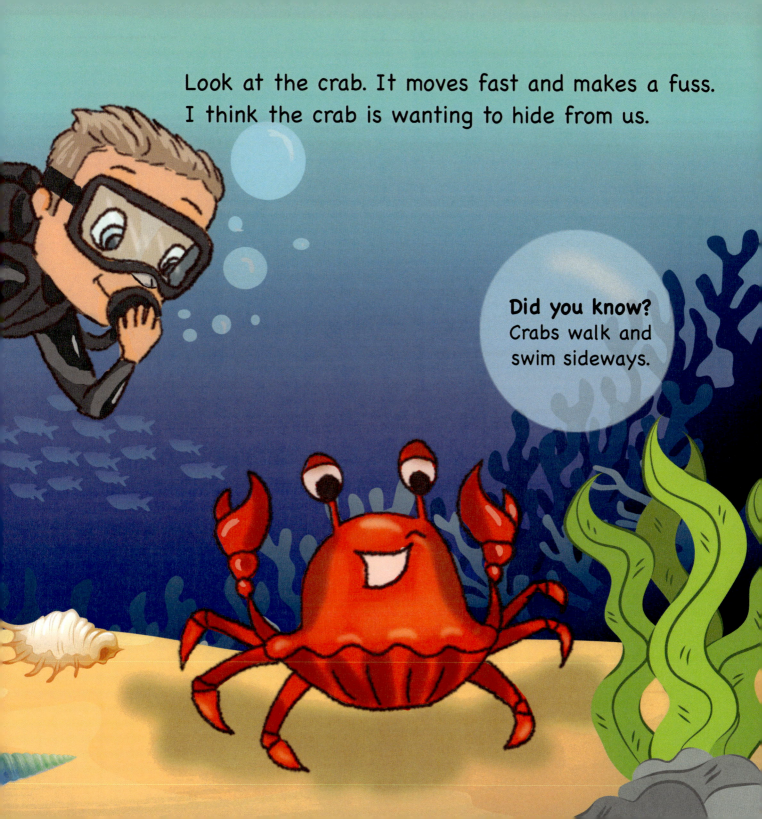

Oh, look over there! Today's our lucky day.
A sea turtle is near and swimming our way.

She's beautiful to watch as she explores the reef.
She's feeding on sponges, chomping plants and leaves.

Did you know? There are 7 species of sea turtles. The largest sea turtle can weigh up to 2,000 pounds.

I turn to my left side and what is that I see?
A big ol' pufferfish is staring back at me.

He is big as a balloon with very small fins.
He looks as if he floats, but pufferfish can swim.

Did you know?
Pufferfish can inflate themselves into a ball shape several times their normal size.

Let's move along and see what else we can explore.
Look! It's an octopus sitting on a cave floor.

He starts to change color from light green to brown.
To hide in plain sight on the rocky coral ground.

I use my fins to kick away. Look what I see.
It's a colorful jellyfish swimming towards me.

Some jellyfish are known to have a painful sting.

So let's move along and let him do his own thing.

Did you know? Jellyfish are made up of 95% water and come in many colors including yellow, pink, blue and purple.

As one glides past, he turns onto his side.
It looks like the stingray is smiling wide.

Did you know? Stingrays are related to sharks and use their fins like wings to move through the water.

I pause as I see what has just crept into view.
It's a shark swimming out in the deep ocean blue.

She swims through the water with confidence and grace.
Let's stop for now. We want to give her some space.

Did you know? There are more than 400 different species of sharks swimming in the ocean.

I check my tank's air level and it's getting low.
This means that now it's time for you and me to go.

We've been underwater exploring for a while.

I hope our adventure today has made you smile.

Did you know? Large coral reefs in our oceans are thousands of years old.

Goodbye for now and thanks for joining me today.
There's no other way I'd rather have spent my day.

I hope you enjoyed our time together under the sea.

Maybe someday you'll become a scuba diver like me!

Made in the USA
Las Vegas, NV
19 May 2023